vanessa

the simple truth
about trust

With simplicity and clarity, Vanessa shares with us her
unique and clever model that shows us how to build
and keep trust in our relationships.

The Simple Truth About Trust

Copyright © 2007 Vanessa Hall

First published 2007 by Entente Pty Limited

Distributed in Australia by: Entente Pty Limited
Level 14, 309 Kent St, Sydney NSW 2000
Ph: 612 9290 8592   Email: info@entente.com.au   Web: www.entente.com.au

For information on bulk orders and other related products see:
www.thetruthabouttrust.com

The Simple Truth About Trust. 1st ed..
ISBN 9780980395310 (pbk.).
1. Trust. 2. Interpersonal relations. I. Title.
Hall, Vanessa (Vanessa Rae), 1969- .

158.2

Design and typeset by David Chambers: www.davidchamberscreative.com.au

Printed and bound by McPherson's Printing Group

"It is impossible to go through life without trust. That is to be imprisoned in the worst cell of all, oneself".

Graham Greene

the ^simple truth about **trust**

the simple *simple*

Trust is at the core of all our **relationships**
– in business and in our personal relationships.

But what is **trust?**

I define trust as our ability to rely on:

- **A person**
- **A company**
- **A product or service**

...to deliver an outcome.

The question is, on who or what do we rely,
and for what outcome?

Let's look at how trust is created and can break down without us even realising it!

My son, Lachlan, who was 9 at the time, brought home a one page description of 'My Mum' that he had made at school for Mother's Day.

Here is a copy of it – see if you can spot the thing that jumped out at me!

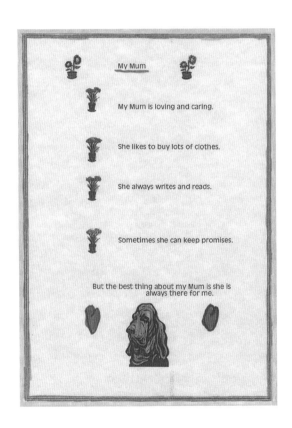

My Mum

My Mum is loving and caring.

She likes to buy lots of clothes.

She always writes and reads.

Sometimes she can keep promises.

But the best thing about my Mum is she is always there for me.

Immediately after the *'Awww, that's lovely. Thank you,'* I then said
*'What do you mean I **sometimes keep promises?'** I* was quite indignant. *'That's not me!'* I thought.

'Well, sometimes you don't keep your promises,' Lachlan said, very matter of fact.

'Can you give me an example?' I was a bit confused at this point.

'Like the other week, you said we might go and see a movie on the weekend and then we didn't go,' he said, with a pout.

'Oh, that's OK. That wasn't really a promise. Was it?'

Lachlan looked at me and said
'I thought it was.'

I thought about what I said and then realised that, whether I meant it as a promise or not, that was how it was **perceived**.

I started thinking about all the times I say things like that,
not only to him, but at work, and to friends. My head started
spinning.
I pulled myself together and asked

'How did that make you feel?'
.......as I reached out to touch his hand.

'I just don't know when I can trust you,' he said.

He looked me squarely in the eyes and I felt like someone reached in and ripped my heart out.

My son taught me a great lesson that day, and it was the start of the development of the model we will look at now.

So, what I realised was that there are a few **core** things that contribute to being able to trust – or not.

And I came up with a very **simple** model, that explains trust.

I draw it like a wall.

The first part of the wall represents our Expectations.

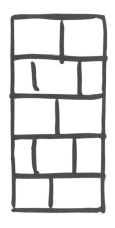

Expectations

We all have **expectations** in every relationship we go into,
and in every interaction with
people, companies, products and services.

Expectations come from:

- Previous experiences we have had
- Things we've seen or heard or read
- Things people tell us
- 'Like' experiences with something similar

For example, in a relationship with your **partner**, you might have expectations that:

- Your anniversary is remembered
- You get to watch the football on Friday night with your mates
- Your partner takes the garbage out

The next part of the wall is our Needs.

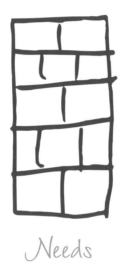

Needs

It's our needs that drive us into all our relationships or interactions – we look for ways to satisfy our needs, every day.

Needs are different from expectations - they are the basic things that we **require** to function, and include things like:

- Need for food, safety and security
- Need for a sense of belonging
- Need for respect
- Need for recognition
- Need for development and growth

The third part of our wall is Promises.

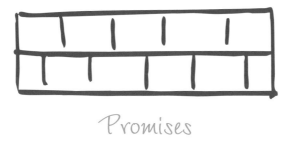

Promises

Now the expectations and needs are **yours** - what you expect and need from your relationship or interaction.

The promises are those made to you by the **other person**, company, product or service.

Promises are made to us **every day**.

They can be implicit or explicit.

The more the promises sound like they will meet our needs, the more likely we will be drawn to that particular person, company, product or service.

Just to clarify –
implicit promises are things that are **suggested**,
but not stated outright.

For example, a company's logo and brand creates implicit promises.

An ad with two happy people advertising a product creates an implicit promise that, if you buy this, you will be happy too.

Or when someone buys you flowers each week for a month,
it creates an implicit promise, and an expectation,
that they will keep buying you flowers!

Explicit promises, on the other hand, are clearly stated and tell you **exactly** what you are going to get.

For example, a company's mission statement and values may often make explicit promises about what it is like to **work** there, and how the staff will behave when you deal with them as a **customer**.

An employment contract is an explicit promise.

A food label is an explicit promise.

Marriage vows are explicit promises.

So, every relationship we go into, and every interaction
we have with a person, company, product or service
is based on these three things:

Our **expectations**, our **needs**, and the **promises** made to us
by the other party.

We call these our

ENPs™

Being able to trust,
our decision to trust, is based on our belief that:

Our **expectations** will be met or managed
Our **needs** will be met, and
the **promises** made to us will be kept.

*The outcome we are relying on others for
is that our ENPs™ are met.*

Our ENP™ wall looks like this:

Now, because trust is something very **fragile**
that can break quite easily...

We represent trust as an **egg**,
So we actually end up with this...

Trust sits on the **balance** of our ENPs™.
If our expectations and needs are not met...

... and the promises made to us are not kept,
then bricks start to **drop** out of the wall.

We all know what happens to Humpty in the nursery rhyme...

"All the King's horses and all the King's men,
couldn't put Humpty together again."

This can happen to **trust**, when the wall breaks down.

For example, we could have Expectations
of our workplace like this:

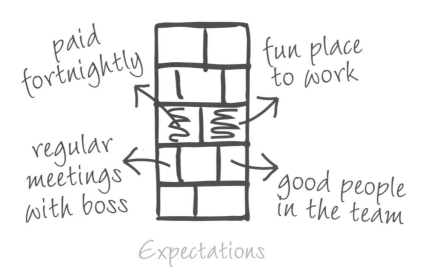

Expectations

The shaded ones are the ones that are most **important** to us.

(These ones break down the wall faster if they are not met
– I know, I had a structural engineer confirm it!)

So, if these expectations **aren't** met,
this is what happens to the wall.

paid
fortnightly

regular
meetings
with boss

fun place
to work

good
people
in the
team

Expectations

The same thing happens to our Needs:

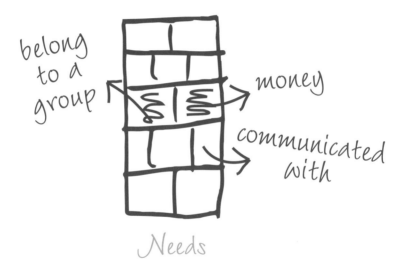

belong to a group

money

communicated with

Needs

belong to a group

communicated with

money

Needs

Implicit promises look like this on our Promises wall:

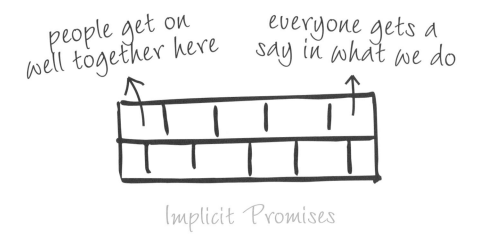

people get on well together here

everyone gets a say in what we do

Implicit Promises

Usually, if these implicit promises are not kept, we get so **annoyed** we just get out of the situation.

We often don't bother to say anything.

Often we **can't** say anything
because the promise was kind of suggested.

It wasn't really definite, but it was still a promise!

Explicit promises look like this on our Promises wall:

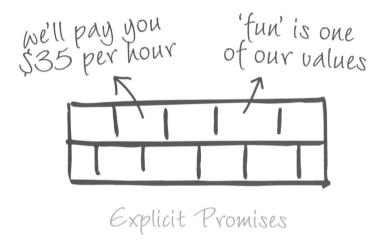

we'll pay you $35 per hour

'fun' is one of our values

Explicit Promises

When **these** ones aren't met, we usually say something.
After all, it was clearly stated, so what were they thinking?

Here's what our whole wall looks like:

TRUST

people get on well together here

$35 per hour

'fun' is one of our values

everyone gets a say in what we do

Promises

paid fortnightly

fun place to work

money

belong to a group

regular meetings with boss

good people in the team

communicated with

Expectations

Needs

So, if **a lot** of these **expectations, needs** and **promises** are not met or kept – look what happens to the wall...

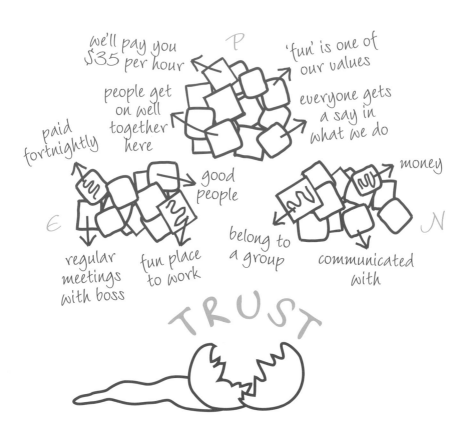

we'll pay you
$35 per hour

P

'fun' is one of
our values

people get
on well
together
here

everyone gets
a say in
what we do

paid
fortnightly

good
people

money

E

belong to
a group

N

regular
meetings
with boss

fun place
to work

communicated
with

TRUST

Sometimes, if some of the 'not so important' ENPs™ are not met, the wall will **crack**, but the trust won't break.

TRUST

people get on well together here

$35 per hour

'fun' is one of our values

everyone gets a say in what we do

Promises

paid fortnightly

fun place to work

money

belong to a group

regular meetings with boss

good people in the team

communicated with

Expectations

Needs

But it won't be very happy either. When this happens, we often feel **disappointed**, confused, and can stop putting effort into the relationship.

What is **critical** to understand if you want
to build trusted relationships
is this...

Be **clear**
about your expectations
and needs of others

Articulate them.

Communicate them whenever you can
so the other person is clear.

Remind them to only
make promises they
can **keep**.

If the person, company, product or service you are dealing with says they **cannot** promise to meet your expectations and needs,
you need to either...

Manage your expectations about the **purpose** of that relationship or interaction or...

Find someone or something else that can.

Your trust is precious, so take good **care** of it.
Don't place it on a wall that is already crumbling.

But remember...

Others will **assess** you
on the same basis,
so...

Find out what others **expect** and **need** of you and only **promise** what you can actually **deliver**.

Trust is so critical to **healthy**,
strong relationships.

We all need to rely on other people.
That's human nature.

When we can trust others, we don't have to worry.
Trust brings **peace** of mind.

Trust is a wonderful **gift**.

When someone trusts you, they are saying:

'I **believe** you will meet my expectations and needs,
and I believe you will keep the promises you made to me.'

That's pretty **special**.

building **trust**

For more information and products to
help you build trust, visit:

www.entente.com.au
www.thetruthabouttrust.com

Thanks and acknowledgments

A big, big thankyou to my son Lachlan who
started me on this journey, and to my wonderful partner Peter
who believes in me, and supports me.

To my younger sister, Belinda, who has spent countless hours
researching so many aspects of trust for me and has stretched
herself to support me.

To Shelley and Leonie who are so excited and passionate
about what we do, they keep the dream alive.

To my friends, Savvas, who has always been there for me,
and Carolyn, who thinks so differently from me
– they both keep me on track

To our Consultants and Friends of Entente,
thanks for getting the news out there!

To **everyone** who reads this book and who changes the way
they build relationships...

Congratulations!

You are making a **difference**!